Leisure Arts 37
Painting
Flowers in
Acrylics
Wendy Jelbert

SEARCH PRESS

Introduction

There is nothing more beautiful than the sight of a field of poppies glowing in the sun, or meadows and gardens full of brightly coloured flowers, and as a subject they offer a rich source of inspiration to the artist. Before you start it is important to observe, study and to practise drawing them. Then you will discover the enjoyment of creating lovely flower pictures.

Most of us are fortunate enough to have easy access to an endless variety of flowers, and we are therefore able to study them at our leisure. They flourish in gardens, window boxes, hedgerows, woods, fields and parks; they can be bought conveniently packaged from shops, street corner sellers or the local supermarket and can be used to grace our homes, delighting us with their glorious colours, designs and shapes. As they are so available, it is hardly surprising that artists are stimulated by their richness and variety.

It is only since the seventeenth century that flowers have really become popular as a focus for artistic interpretation. It is worthwhile visiting exhibitions of flower paintings if you have the time. I like studying Jan Van Huysum's enchanting pictures which can be seen at the National Gallery, London; or the rose paintings of Fantin-Latour that I have discovered in my local municipal gallery in Southampton. I also love the less formal flower studies by Beatrix Potter. Artists interpret flowers in different ways and it is up to you to find your own way of expressing their colours, shapes and form.

Acrylic paints are an ideal medium for painting flowers. Their quick drying qualities can be used to advantage and with practise you will be able to apply successive transparent washes of subtly varying colours

Unusual props can be used as supports for clinging or climbing plants. Here convolvulus twists and turns around an old wooden post. (see page 10).

to their leaves and petals. Also wonderful textural effects can be created using thick impasto work. Grasping the potential of acrylic paint can be great fun!

To freeze the transitory beauty of flowers and to be able to capture their moment of perfection in your sketchbook or painting you will need patiently acquired skills. I hope I can convey these skills to you in this book. It is important to draw and paint as many different types of flowers as you can. With observation and practise you will discover the endless delights of painting flowers.

Materials

One of the characteristics of acrylics is that they can be successfully applied to a wide range of surfaces. I mainly use a prepared canvas board, fine oil paper, or 140 lb rough watercolour paper. When using paper, I anchor it down on to a drawing board with masking tape.

You will need a range of hog-hair, ox-hair, squirrel-hair and nylon brushes. The size and shape will depend on the style and scale of your work. When using acrylics I use the same brushes for my oils and watercolours so I don't have to buy a whole new set. Hog-hair brushes are generally used for applying thicker paint; the softer brushes, like ox-hair, squirrel-hair and nylon are used for thinner applications of paint, and are suitable for the watercolour technique. I also use a palette knife for applying thicker paint. Acrylic gel can be useful here too. It is available in tubes, like toothpaste. I mix it up with the paint to bulk it up and it increases translucency and retards the drying rate to some degree.

Masking fluid can produce some interesting special effects. I use a ruling pen to apply the fluid because it can be adjusted to draw lines of varying widths. Areas of white can be created by applying masking fluid to the bare surface before laying a wash.

Gloss and matt glaze mediums when added to the water will allow the paint to flow more easily; this is especially useful when applying washes over large areas. As a secondary function, they can be mixed together to form a lovely "satin" varnish.

Retarder extends the setting time of acrylics and when mixed with the paints it allows them to stay moist, so they are workable for a longer period of time.

There are many types of commercial palettes available. You can buy disposable palettes which are useful for outdoor work, or there are the traditional wooden or plastic varieties. However, the palette most favoured by my students consists of a plastic container with a transparent plastic top. It measures 23 cm × 35.5 cm (9 in × 14 in) and has disposable paper linings which, when moistened, keeps the paint workable for longer periods. Indoors or out it is quite excellent. If you like to keep things simple and inexpensive, a dinner plate will do! A pottery or porcelain surface is easy to keep clean. If the paint becomes dry and hard, just soak the plate in hot water.

The choice of easel is mainly personal and possibly a matter of compromise. Mine is reasonably light in weight, but sturdily made from steel. It can be adjusted for use on a table and is steady enough to be used for location work.

For sketching I use a soft rubber and a spiral bound watercolour pad. I also use a cartridge paper drawing book with a hard cover which forms a solid base when working outside. I prefer to use a variety of pencils, and include in my range a 5B solid graphite and a soft water soluble pencil, and I also work with pencils of varying softness within the HB – 6B range. It is important to keep your pencils sharp, either with a pencil sharpener, or a craft knife.

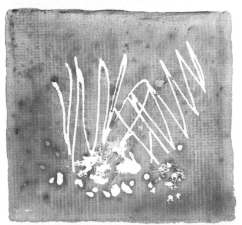

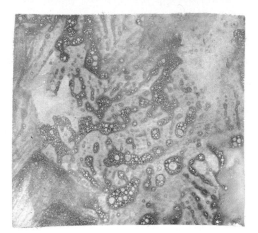

Techniques

Acrylics are enormously versatile if used to their fullest extent. I find exercises are an essential ingredient in obtaining a visual vocabulary. Only by practising with the paints and the colours can you improve your painting skills. Opposite I illustrate several simple exercises for you to try. Experiment with different surfaces, such as canvas or acrylic board, or as I have here with 140 lb watercolour paper.

Top left: on a wetted surface I drop different colours and watch how they bleed together. This technique produces a soft, misty impression.

Top right: a rich textured surface can be created by mixing colours with gel medium and applying them over a basic wash with a palette knife.

Centre left: I apply lines and dots of masking fluid to the bare surface and allow it to dry thoroughly before painting over it with a wash. When dry, the masking fluid can be rubbed off, leaving the underlying paper showing through.

Centre right: to give the surface an exciting visual impact, I break it up with stabbing lines, streaks, dots and washes of varying colours. Try this out several times, as the effects you can achieve are limitless.

Bottom left: I overlay violet with a scumble of yellow ochre, allowing the violet to peep through the added layers. This makes the surface of the painting "sing" with patterns of colour. In the past many artists have used burnt sienna in the same way as I have used the violet, placing it under landscape paintings.

Bottom right: I mix watery acrylic paint with matt or gloss medium and apply it briskly to the surface with a hog-hair brush. Air bubbles are captured in the paint; this interesting effect can be used when painting foliage and wood.

Petals and flower heads

It is important to understand the structure of any flower you are recreating. The diversity of their shapes, tones, textures and colours have to be studied and sketched in some depth before starting to paint. A finished painting cannot be first class if the underlying draughtsmanship is poor. Drawing and painting are therefore inseparable. You can only capture the fragility of your subject by drawing it correctly in the beginning. Developing and clarifying this understanding will take time and effort and you will most certainly regret your haste if you try to skip this essential stage.

Choose a small assortment of petals and flower heads in a variety of colours and shapes, (see page 6). Now, with 2B and 6B pencils, sketch them on to a sheet of cartridge paper, or use your sketchbook. My class students will readily dissect a flower head so they can study its structure in detail. They will then draw the single head from several different angles. The confidence gained helps them tremendously when more complex flower studies are tackled.

Flower forms can be recognised in terms of a series of geometrical shapes. Most are based on cylinders, pyramids, spheres and cones. Below, in fig.a, I show how a shallow cone forms the basis of a simple daisy. In fig.b I show how the bluebell can be based on a simple pyramid. A compound flower, such as a fuchsia, or the daffodil shown in fig.c, can be constructed from a combination of cylindrical and conical shapes; the smaller forms slot into, or are enclosed by, the outer ones. Study the flowers in your own garden and practise extracting framework sketches of their structure. Simple blooms can be analysed in this way. But if you want to paint flowers with a more complex structure, you will have to rely on your own powers of observation.

fig. a

fig. b

fig. c

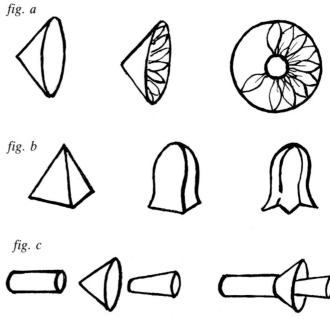

When you are satisfied with your drawing, it is time to start to experiment with your colours. With or without a preliminary drawing, paint the petals and flower heads using the illustrations as a guide.

Leaves

Leaves are an integral part of the whole flower, and therefore require the same attention to detail as the flower heads and petals. You must also take special care to ensure that the proportions of the flowers to the leaves are accurate, or the finished painting just won't look right.

Whatever the nature of the leaf you are studying, its basic form can be analysed as a simple shape. I have already shown this when describing the petals and flower heads opposite. Circles, triangles or rectangles can be used to build up the basic form.

Once you have established the correct design, you have to then consider the possibility of drawing or painting several or many leaves. Their massed shapes can be an essential dramatic foil to your flower study. Rhythmical lines can be created by arching and pulling the leaves in various directions.

First of all, choose several leaves of different sizes, shapes and colours, and practise drawing them individually before starting to paint. As well as ready mixed greens, such as viridian, Hookers green and olive green, you will need to mix some of your own using blues and yellows. Below I discuss how you can construct a simple exercise which should help you to solve any problems you may have with leaves and foliage.

Take a clean piece of paper; gather together your ready mixed greens and mix some of your own using blues and yellows. Place these colours down the left-hand side of your paper. Then place crimson, burnt sienna, orange, pink and deep purple in a row along the top. Now modify each green in turn with each of the top colours. Mix equal amounts of each colour in all cases, working through the whole block. You will discover some lovely subtle and useful greens. If a darker green is required, thicker paint is needed.

Props

Unless you are using a purely illustrative style, you will probably want to include some sort of accessories in your flower picture to create atmosphere, stability, or even decoration. If you use a container, choose it carefully so that its shape and colour will harmonise with your chosen flowers. Be imaginative; don't always use the same one. An enterprising flower painter will start a collection of suitable objects that will complement his or her work.

As well as the container, consider the addition of other props – perhaps a mirror to create another dimension, or a shelf that could break the blankness of a simple flat base into two levels. There are many possibilities.

Glass can be quite difficult to interpret as it absorbs and reflects surrounding colours. In the painting at the top of this page there is an intriguing distortion of the jar's contents. Before you start on a subject like this, observe these effects carefully: the interlocking areas of colour, tone and form combine like a jigsaw puzzle. Analyse them in your own way. The highlights in a scene like this may not be as white as you may at first think. Do not make them too stark.

In the painting below, I have placed two carnations on a white lace trimmed tablecloth. You will note that I have toned the tablecloth down and introduced soft, interpreted reflections of pinks and blues.

I start by drawing the carnations and basic form of the lace patterns with a 3B pencil. Then, using a ruling pen, I apply the masking fluid to the intricate parts of the lace and I highlight the flowers. When the fluid is dry, I paint in thin washes of violet and blue over the background, the shadowed areas of the cloth and the foreground. I gently deepen the tones of the lace that lie beneath the carnation in the foreground. When the masking fluid is removed, the lace pattern appears slightly more prominent than the surrounding areas. Finally, using my rigger brush I add more detail to the lace patterns with purples and blues.

Urns and tubs

Here I concentrate on outdoor subjects. You should be able to visualise your chosen flowers in a variety of settings – primroses on a patio in a terracotta pot, or nestling in a hedgerow for instance. With practise, you will soon be able to imagine these location cameos into which your flowers can be set. Look around you. Seek out interesting nooks and crannies and record them in your sketchbook for future reference.

Both the pictures on this page are from my sketchbook. When deciding on your container remember that it must act as a foil, quietly complementing, and never dominating the plant it holds. Let us start with the weathered stone urn. I pencil in its basic shape and surface design. I then apply an initial wash of diluted yellow ochre and while it is still moist I use a toothbrush to 'splatter' olive green and light red in small areas, giving a realistic pitted and rough look. With a rigger brush I complete the detail of the pot's surface decoration. Here I use olive green and crimson in the shadowed area and the recesses of the scrolled and fluted forms. The highlights can now be superimposed with dryer white and crimson plus a touch of yellow.

Although the tub is easier to draw than the urn, it is still important to be careful with the drawing. The bands that bind the tub together must all follow the same gentle curve. Here I have arranged the flowers so they tumble over the edge of the tub to soften the hardness of its edges. This also helps the blooms to retain their dominance over the container. I use blue, light red and olive green for the bands and paint in the grain with a rigger brush using dark crimson and olive green.

Using natural surroundings

You will have to become a keen opportunist to capture some of the beauty and delights of nature: a bee alighting on a flower petal, a butterfly teetering on a bud, or a spider's web glistening like glass.

Here I have incorporated a web into one of my bramble paintings. It is highlighted against a background of dark foliage, part reflecting the light. I found the easiest way in which to tackle this complicated web was, after the initial drawing, to home in with a drawing pen and painstakingly cover the detail with masking fluid. When it was dry I painted in the background. Then, making quite sure that the background was dry, I briskly rubbed off the masking fluid, uncovering the virgin

white paper beneath. A transparent wash assured that this blended gently with the surrounding areas.

Another alternative is to paint in the background first, then when this is dry, the web can be constructed over the top with a rigger brush, using white paint.

The 'props' that really delight me are those that are unusual or hidden away; the fence, the broken gate post or the dead stalk supporting a clinging or climbing plant like the honeysuckle or ivy. In the picture on page 2, I have painted some convolvulus twisting around an old post complete with rusty catch! Search for intriguing and unusual frameworks for your plants and practise drawing and painting them in your sketchbook.

W. Talbot

Roses

Size: 28 cm × 28 cm (10½ in × 10½ in)
Paper: watercolour paper 140 lb
Brushes: no. 6 round-headed nylon, no. 1 rigger, 1 cm (½ in) flat-headed squirrel-hair.
Colours: vermilion, yellow ochre, white, Hookers green, light red, crimson, ultramarine blue.

The rose has an irresistable charm. It is a sentimental messenger awakening feelings of love, beauty and peace and the intricacy of its 'gathered skirts' offers a glorious array of shapes, styles and colours. This delightful and powerful flower is surely a temptation for the flower painter.

Amongst the common types of rose which are a delight to paint are singles, ramblers, climbers, briars, hybrid teas, floribundas and miniatures. It can be quite a problem knowing where to start, but I suggest you begin by sketching the flower in its natural habitat as I have in the sketch on this page. This will help you to become familiar with its characteristics. If roses are not in season, I often use the beautifully realistic silk flowers that are available today. They are an ideal substitute and have the added advantage of never wilting.

Here and on the next page, I illustrate how to build up the head of a single rose. Select your own rose and practise drawing it from different angles, perhaps including a few leaves, thus preparing the way for tackling the rose arch in the final painting on page 13.

Stage 1 (*see page 12*)
With the rigger brush and a little ultramarine blue, I roughly sketch in the rose head.

Stage 2 (*see page 12*)
Changing to the squirrel-hair brush, I apply a watery wash to the flower head using yellow ochre, with light red and vermilion run in; I allow the separate colours to disperse softly. To create a contrast, before the colours dry, more paint can be added to some petal edges. I paint in the base of the flower head and the stalk using Hookers green and light red.

Stage 3 (*see page 12*)
Using the nylon brush, I now add the deeper shadows with a mixture of crimson and Hookers green. It is important to let some of the background wash 'glow' through these layers which adds a feeling of 'warmth' to the flower. I paint in the lighter areas, where the petals are folding over, with crimson and white, and I darken the centre with crimson and a touch of Hookers green to create a sense of depth. Finally I add a touch of yellow ochre, Hookers green and crimson to the base of the flower head and stalk.

Stage 4 – the finished painting see overleaf

11

Stage 1

Stage 2

Stage 3

Stage 4 – the finished painting

Now you are ready to start on the painting of the rose
arch. It will need careful planning in the drawing stage
and the work that you have already done will be of great
value.

I paint in the wooden arch with a variation of yellow
ochre, Hookers green and light red, drawing in the bark
texture with my rigger brush. The wood texturing can
also be painted in as suggested on page 4 (bottom right).
I paint in the leaves using a range of ready-mixed greens,
with mixes of blue and yellow, and the flower heads as I
show on this page.

Because acrylics are quick drying and they also have
the quality, if necessary, of being able to obscure
underlying paint, they are ideal for massed areas of
flower heads and foliage. Later details can be easily
added without the fear of disturbing previous work.
Likewise, shadows can be applied with a translucent
wash of crimson and ultramarine blue to give the
composition a feeling of depth and realism.

Stage 4 – the finished painting

Backgrounds

I believe that this section will be of special interest to every painter. There are many subjects (not only flowers) that require the careful choice of a sympathetic background. Your flower painting will have more impact and will give you greater satisfaction if you can successfully overcome the difficulties of selecting the content, tone and colour.

It will not do to just slap any old colour on to the background, hoping for the best! The background provides the setting that will embrace and enhance your subject. It will influence every step you take in the progression of your painting.

The foreground objects must have an affinity with the background and in any painting you should always develop your background and foreground as one unit. This allows the scene to unfold and progress as a whole. In many cases, the blooms and the background can be painted over with the same first wash, exuding a feeling of oneness. The background must not merely surround the flowers, but must contribute some atmosphere and sparkle of its own.

The pictures opposite show the same bunch of white tulips with different backgrounds. The top left painting is a study in contrasts. The tulip heads in the light of the window appear darker than those in the adjacent painting. These appear to have been made lighter by the darker fabric behind, even though in both paintings the tulips are the same colour. In a multiple subject like a bunch of flowers, the blooms can be remarkably alike in colour and tone. This technique can therefore force much needed extra contrast and variety.

In the top right painting I have simplified the tulips and placed them in front of a brightly coloured material. The lines and flow of the design form an intricate pattern in which the tulips are of secondary importance.

This is a useful exercise for the student. The use of an extravagant background will help you to select the more important features and leave out others when tackling a scene which would otherwise be cluttered and overbearing. Acrylics are excellent for this kind of experimentation. Layers can be added, mistakes obscured with white and quickly repainted, and delicate washes applied to soften and diffuse hard edges. The speed with which images can be created and then demolished at a whim is incredible!

In the bottom left painting I have placed the tulips in a natural sunlit setting. If you are lucky enough to have them growing in your garden, then painting them 'in situ' is even better. All the ingredients are there just waiting for your attention – atmosphere, lighting and background. In my painting the character of the setting is sufficiently subdued in colour and tone so as to avoid the flowers being dominated. Notice how the sunlight throws the luxuriant leaves into bright silhouette. The patch of shadow in the background helps to give this impression.

The final painting, bottom right, is a perfectly traditional setting. The tulips are displayed against the restrained pattern of a length of material which is arranged in attractive folds in the background. These folds should not conflict with the fundamental compositional forms of your flowers, but should harmonise with them.

Opposite: The same bunch of white tulips is portrayed in these four pictures, but each has a different background. Notice how the colours of the tulips appear to change. In a subject like this the colours and tones of the flowers can be very similar, so backgrounds can provide much needed contrast and variety.

Poppies and daisies

Size: 39 cm × 27 cm (15½ in × 10½ in)
Paper: watercolour paper 140 lb
Brushes: no. 6 hog-hair, no. 8 flat-headed ox or squirrel-hair, no. 1 nylon rigger
Colours: olive green, crimson, vermilion, ultramarine blue, white, cadmium yellow, yellow ochre
Other materials: soft pencil, masking fluid, acrylic gel, ruling pen, an old toothbrush

Scarlet poppies, fragile, silky and radiant in a haze of small white daisies are an ever-popular subject for flower painters. They are fascinating, not only because of their glorious brilliance of colour and their delicate texturing, but also for the feeling of countryside romanticism they evoke for an age that is slowly, but surely, fading. The versatile qualities of acrylic paints make them the ideal medium for translating this compelling subject into a workable painting. I use both the 'wet-in-wet' and 'oil' technique, and take advantage of the inherent quick drying qualities of acrylics to exploit this exciting medium to its fullest extent.

I often find in my classes that the complete beginner, who may be less prejudiced and more adventurous, often has an advantage over the skilled painter who may be burdened with preconceived ideas. The beginner's fresh, even naive approach, may result in an unexpectedly original study. My suggested methods in all of these step-by-step projects will provide a useful framework to start with, but I hope that, in time and with practise, you will develop a style and method of your own.

Stage 1

First I establish the two main poppy heads, drawing them in with a soft pencil. I then add the buds, stalks, foliage and daisies. Next I apply masking fluid to the outlines of all these features where maximum brilliance will be needed.

Stage 2

First I mix two dull greens (olive green and light red, ultramarine blue and yellow ochre). I wet the paper surface thoroughly and, using the ox or squirrel-hair brush, I apply the two greens to the appropriate areas, allowing them to mix and run into one another in places. As they dry, I quickly darken some of the foreground foliage, beginning to give it form. I drop vermilion and cadmium yellow into the poppy heads.

Stage 3

I add the two background poppies in low key while the greens are still wet, and using ultramarine and white I paint in the small glimpse of sky. This is important, so if your paint has dried re-wet it. This lovely wet-in-wet technique produces a soft and fluid image which is so important in the early stages of a painting. If you are too 'tight' in your approach at this stage your painting will look overworked and lifeless. Next, using the hog-hair brush and olive green, I emphasise more detail in the foliage patterns. Finally, I rub off the masking fluid.

Stage 4

The stark white shapes now revealed are gently blended into their surroundings. I use cadmium yellow and ultramarine for the foliage, vermilion for the poppies and a translucent wash of ultramarine for the daisy heads. I then add the final highlights with a mixture of white and the base colour to introduce light and sparkle to the work.

At this stage the painting is almost finished. The important balance of colours and tones have been basically established and I am ready for the finishing touches. I restate and strengthen the middle distance and foreground with olive green and acrylic gel, to give a feeling of depth and mystery. Then, using a rigger brush and a mixture of crimson and white, I build up the crinkled texture of the petals with short line strokes radiating from the centres. These centres and the stamens are delicately painted in using light and dark greens.

Stage 5 – the finished painting see overleaf

Stage 1

Stage 2

Stage 3

Stage 4

Stage 5 – the finished painting

Using the techniques I have explained in Stages 1–4, you can now build up this final composition. Taking further advantages of the versatile qualities of acrylics, I include some more ideas in this larger and more complicated picture. I paint a 'misting' translucent wash of yellow ochre over the farthest poppies to lessen their impact and push them farther into the distance. To enliven the foreground expanse with more variety and texture, I splatter in dark greens against the light yellow on the right, and light greens against the darker accents on the left with an old toothbrush. The tall, erect corns (cadmium yellow and white), the grasses and slender stems with their buds, need to intertwine and intersect the whole composition to create a more haphazard and natural environment.

Stage 5 – the finished painting

* Stage 1

Clematis

Size: 27 cm × 27 cm (10½ in × 10½ in)
Paper: fine oil paper
Brushes: no. 4 hog-hair, no. 8 squirrel, nylon rigger brush
Colours: ultramarine blue, crimson, white, yellow ochre, light red, Hookers green
Other materials: soft pencil, an old rag

This queen of flowers, majestic yet modest, tumbles and cascades over buildings, dissolving hard edges with a colourful softness; it graces arches, walls and fences, offering the artist an exquisite array of colours, shapes, sizes and foliage patterns.

Here I have chosen to paint a purple 'Lasurstern' against a dark yellow brick wall. The colour and texture of the background flatters and highlights the attractiveness of the flowers.

As usual, before commencing I establish the correct proportions and compositional rhythms of the flower in a preliminary drawing. It is always best, where possible, to sketch from nature and to explore just one flower from different angles. You can then refer to these sketches at a later date and use them as a guide should you want to paint a more complicated composition like the final painting of the clematis on page 22. After all, you may feel inspired to paint a clematis in the depths of winter!

Stage 1

I arrange a single clematis bloom so that the detail of its

20

Stage 2

blue, crimson and white. At this point I intensify the background with light red and yellow ochre, again using the piece of rag. I use Hookers green and crimson for the veins of the petals then I change to a rigger brush and, with green and violet, I apply the bud and leaf markings.

Stage 3 – the finished painting (*see page 22*)

I have created a more interesting composition in this final stage and following the methods I have just outlined you should be able to build up your own picture.

I give the bricks their texture by dabbing them with the rag which I crumple and wet with light red and green. I use white to indicate the cement pointing, then glaze it with a transparent yellow ochre, warming and unifying it with the bricks. These glazes, or transparent washes, are a useful quality in acrylics. The paint can be mixed either with water or acrylic medium (gloss or matt) to produce a gentle wash of colour that will harmonise and soften even a discordant work, enhancing and reducing the colours it covers.

Here I use a glaze, not only on the brickwork, but also in some of the shaded areas behind the flower heads. I make a sufficiently dark mix of Hookers green, light red and blue, so that the shadows merge with the background leaves, introducing an ambiguous quality. Using the squirrel-hair brush and the rigger brush I add the light green intertwining stems and graceful leaves on top of the shaded area. The deep accents and veins decorating the petal are painted in using purple and green.

Finally, using the rigger brush, I touch in the centres of the flowers with yellow ochre and white.

structure and character can be clearly seen, then I do a quick pencil sketch of the flower. Using the squirrel-hair brush, I apply a purple wash (ultramarine blue and crimson) to the petal area, and green (Hookers green and light red) to the bud, leaf and stem. With a piece of rag, I 'paint' in a light red and purple background.

Stage 2

This is the part of the painting I really enjoy. The picture begins to come to life even before the details are added. It is an important stage because subtle variations in the tones of the main colour give the painting that essential second dimensional feel that is completely lacking in the first stage. Using the hog-hair brush I establish the individual petal forms with a mixture of ultramarine

Stage 3 – the finished painting

Dandelions and thistles

Size: 28 cm × 28 cm (10½ in × 10½ in)
Paper: watercolour paper 140 lb
Brushes: no. 6 hog-hair, no. 8 ox-hair, no. 1 nylon rigger
Colours: white, yellow ochre, Hookers green, cadmium yellow, ultramarine blue
Other materials: palette knife, masking fluid, old toothbrush

Often a painter will want to include two or more different flowers in a picture, but it may not always be possible to find them naturally growing together, or forming a suitable composition. I often take bicycle rides through my local lanes seeking inspiration and new ideas. I make mental notes of any attractive or promising places that are worth a second visit, especially if there are plants growing there that will blossom later in the season. On one such adventure I made two

sketches shown on this page; they gave me the inspiration for the final painting shown on page 25. I was fascinated by the golden yellow dandelions with their delicate seed heads like misty orbs, and by the wonderful way they contrasted with the tall spikey thistle with its violet blue flower.

Stage 1 (*see page 24*)

I use a soft pencil to sketch in this fairly complicated flower arrangement, referring to my original sketches as a guide, and splatter masking fluid on to the three dandelion clocks with an old toothbrush. A wash of yellow ochre is applied to the background, leaving the white seed heads untouched. Using the squirrel-hair brush I block in the blue sky, then place the leaf shadows in the foreground with yellow ochre and Hookers green. Working quickly, I paint in the yellow dandelion heads,

Stage 1

Stage 2

allowing them to blend into the still wet background colour.

Using white I quickly glaze pale circles over the darker area on the right to represent the seed heads. I accentuate the bud on the left and a few stems with Hookers green, then paint over the dried masking fluid with a little green. Finally, I dot in the thistle heads in the background with Hookers green and light red.

Stage 2

The composition is now established but the bands of texture require more detail. I enrich the dark thistles with ultramarine and light red and complete the spikey decoration with the rigger brush. As I feel the foreground could be darkened a little, I block in some leaf shapes using a mixture of light red, blue and green. I now rub off the masking fluid and paint in the delightful pink stems of the dandelions.

Stage 3 – the finished painting

Now I have to draw in the final details and tie up the rhythmical tonal areas of the picture. With a glaze made up of Hookers green, ultramarine and a touch of light red, I cover the middle distance, bringing into sharp focus those brilliant yellow heads with the now shady depths beneath. Using a palette knife I apply yellow ochre to the flower heads in regimented lines, giving texture and form to the individual petals. In the foreground the large leaves are reinstated with the palette knife and the leaves behind are made to recede by painting over them with their own colour mixed with yellow ochre. I use the ox-hair brush for this. Finally I carefully add tiny blue and white star shapes to the delicate seed heads with the rigger brush.

Do not completely cover the original yellow ochre wash, but allow small specks of it to gleam through. This will enliven the surface and give it a unifying warmth.

Stage 3 – the finished painting

Bluebells

Size: 27 cm × 27 cm (10½ in × 10½ in)
Paper: watercolour paper 140 lb
Brushes: no. 4 hog-hair, no. 8 squirrel-hair, no. 1 rigger
Colours: ultramarine blue, light green and olive green, cadmium yellow, light red, white, crimson
Other materials: fine felt tipped pen, palette knife.

I find that one of the joys of being a painter is that I can lose myself in nature's enchanting hidden-away places. I stumbled across such a place while out walking in the Forest of Beer one bright spring morning and was inspired to paint the picture on page 28. Gentle sunlight filtering through the trees highlighted the tranquility of

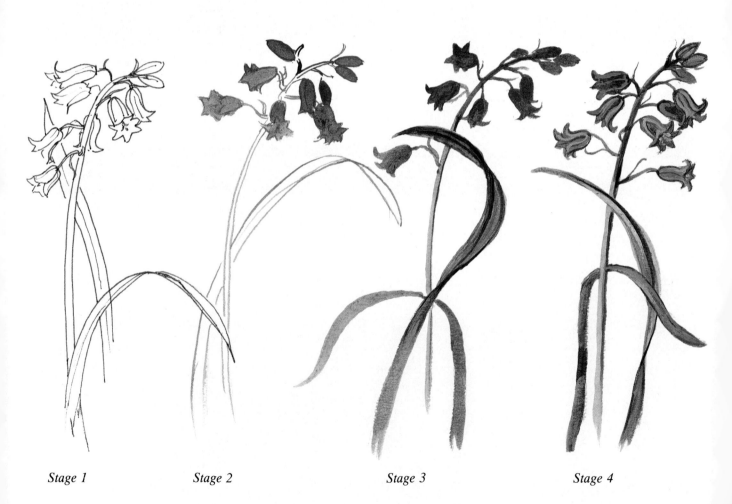

Stage 1   *Stage 2*   *Stage 3*   *Stage 4*

the wood, which was garlanded with a dazzling profusion of sweet scented bluebells. Everywhere fragrance filled the air and the trees cast their shadows across the path forming an interesting pattern as it meandered into the distance.

My first response to a lovely scene like this is always an emotional one, but when I begin to sketch I often find that the 'picture' is not so easy to capture on paper. So I resort to using a 'viewfinder'.

A viewfinder can be easily made on the spot from a piece of card – or use a sheet of paper from your sketchbook. Cut, or tear, a rectangular window, the same proportions as your sketchbook. When you look through this window it is far easier to choose a balanced composition because all unwanted areas are masked off. Identify the ingredients that first arouse your interest and keep them in mind throughout your project.

With a 'busy' scene like the bluebell wood you are bound to make a few mistakes. Don't worry. All painters slip up now and again! Acrylics are very forgiving when mistakes occur. Because of their quick-drying and opaque qualities errors can be easily covered over.

You need to constantly practise your drawing, so don't start to paint straightaway. Study the individual flowers carefully – even count the number of flowers on each stem and the number of petals on each flower.

Stages 1 and 2 (opposite)

First of all I practise drawing the flower using a fine felt tipped pen. Then, when I am satisfied with the drawing, I mix ultramarine and crimson to make a range of blue and purple tones and, using the squirrel-hair brush, I outline the leaves, flowers and stem, and wash in the bell shapes.

Stage 3

Using the same mix, but with more crimson than blue, I darken some of the bells further. I paint in the stems and leaves with light green, olive green and blue.

Stage 4

I lighten the leaves in places with cadmium yellow and olive green. I allow the darker colour of the veins to peep through from the previous stage, in the same way as the oil painting technique of light on dark. In a similar way I complete the flowers with ultramarine, crimson and white.

Stage 5 – the finished painting (See page 28)

If you can find an idyllic woodland glade near your home, all the better. You can really enjoy this project. Otherwise you will have to use my picture as a guide, together with a little imagination! When you paint the bluebells into the landscape take care to avoid flat, regimented blue patches which will look very dull. Here I use a palette knife on the foreground clusters and on the sunlit leaves hovering above them. The broken sunlight falling on the flowers below forms bands of highlights, which I interpret with a variety of brush strokes. With the rigger brush I dot in an impression of the more distant bells and with tapering sweeps indicate the leaves. Using the hog-hair brush I make both short stabbing strokes and longer strokes for the path and the tree bark texture. For dramatic effect I exaggerate the depth of the shadow with a darker glaze of ultramarine and olive green, using the squirrel-hair brush. It is worth mentioning that many artists will over-emphasize certain features to create, enhance and spotlight a vital element.

Cow Parsley

Size: 27 cm × 27 cm (10½ in × 10½ in)
Paper: watercolour paper 140 lb
Brushes: no. 10 hog-hair, no. 4 squirrel-hair, no. 1 rigger
Colours: light red, olive green, yellow ochre, ultramarine blue, deep violet, white
Other materials: black waterproof ink to sharpen the detail.

The sheer elegance of cow parsley, this true proclaimer of spring, never fails to inspire in me a feeling of real tenderness. The delicate lacy haze hovers gently above hedgerows, grassy banks and byways. Like rivulets, the softness of its flowers swirls around trees and gateways, forming interesting patterns and focal points for the artist in search of inspiration.

For this demonstration I use the two photographs seen here, integrating them to create the final painting on page 31. From the photograph below, I extract the trees, elaborate on them, and then balance the composition by placing the clump of ivy on the left in the middle distance. I then use the close-up photograph as reference for the plants in the foreground. If you only have limited time on an outing, a camera and a sketchbook can be used to provide a wealth of material which can be referred to all year round. I often staple

any photographs I take into my sketchbook, along with the relevant sketches.

Stage 1 (*overleaf*)

I omit the pencil drawing stage this time and, on wetted paper, go straight to work with the hog-hair brush and apply a wash of yellow ochre. Into this I drop variations of a mix of olive green and violet, cooled with a touch of ultramarine. I also add thick blobs of white that bleed attractively into the darker surrounding colours to form the basis of the cow parsley shapes. Next, while the colours are still wet, I apply black ink to the central area,

Stage 1

Stage 2

priming it to take the lighter details of the plant in the next stage. If you succeed in doing all this quickly enough, I hope you will discover for yourself how spontaneous and free this wet-in-wet technique can be.

Stage 2

I now start to paint in the details. Using light green and the rigger brush, I add the slim stems which criss-cross each other. I draw in the central darker flower head using pen and ink; some delicate penwork is also added to the lighter flowers around it. Using the squirrel-hair brush I paint in the feathered cow parsley leaves with olive green and yellow ochre. I add touches of white to the lacy flower heads.

Stage 3 – the finished painting

To create the final painting I use all the techniques described in stages 1 and 2. As I lay down the first wash of yellow ochre, I add an expanse of ultramarine and white to the sky area and, before it dries, quickly paint in the distant misty trees with blue and light red. The two dominant trees are embellished with ivy, using a variety of dots and stabbing marks in varying hues of light red and pale yellow-greens. A band of light green is ribboned through the background, gently silhouetting the middle distant features. Notice the lively dots and streaks of light red that are flicked into the grasses. They break the monotony of a picture that could otherwise be too green.

Stage 3 – the finished painting

First Published in Great Britain 1990
Search Press Ltd,
Wellwood, North Farm Road,
Tunbridge Wells, Kent TN2 3DR

Text, paintings and drawings by Wendy Jelbert

U.S. Artists Materials Trade Distributors:
Winsor & Newton, Inc.
11, Constitution Avenue, P.O. Box 1396, Piscataway,
NJ 0885-1396

Canadian Distributors:
Anthes Universal Limited
341 Heart Lake Road South, Brampton, Ontario L6W 3K8

Australian Distributors:
Jasco Pty Limited
937-941 Victoria Road, West Ryde, N.S.W 2114

New Zealand Distributors:
Caldwell Wholesale Limited
Wellington and Auckland

*The author would like to thank her husband Roger for the many
hours of help he gave her during the preparation of this book.*

ISBN 0 85532 649 2

Typeset by Scribe Design, 123 Watling Street, Gillingham, Kent
Made and Printed in Spain by A.G Elkar S. Coop. Bilbao-12